...NOT KNOWING THEM IS DANGEROUS

6 Alarming Things Every Teenager Must know About Social Media

CHUKWUMA GORDIAN

6 ALARMING THINGS EVERY TEENAGER MUST KNOW ABOUT SOCIAL MEDIA
By Chukwuma Gordian

Copyright © 2021 Chukwuma Gordian

ISBN: 978-978-990-160-9

Published by:
Stay Alive Int'l
Beseech Concepts Suite: 11, Olowu Street, Ikeja, Lagos
stayaliveintl@gmail.com
+234 809 822 0369, 802 930 9859

For:
Chukwuma Gordian
hello@chumagordian.com
www.chumagordian.com

DEDICATION

This book is dedicated to every African teenager who is willing to make a difference in this generation.

CONTENT

Dedication iii

Read This First: Information To Reader.............................6

One:
What Exactly Is Social Media?.....................................10

Two:
How To Become A Teenage
Social Media Influencer... 46

Three:
How To Cultivate A Good
 Social Media Self-Esteem..64

Four:
4 Negative Social Media Influence
You Should Avoid...73

Five:
5 Ways To Appear Responsible
On Social Media..84

Six:
10 Social Media Ethics You Must
Know As A Teenager...92

"The world has never been distracted as they are today. Same way, the world has never been connected as they are today. In these distractions and connections are opportunities, but until you see the opportunities, you will remain distracted."
**--- Chukwuma Gordian
(Mr. Solution)**

READ THIS FIRST

Dear friend,
Your decision to read this book might turn out to be one of the best decisions you've ever made.

This book became necessary because I have you in mind. I want the best from you. I really want to see you at the top.

I noticed a rapid increase in the use of social media among teenagers like you, not also forgetting the positive and the negative exposure it can give. Social media today is among the key things that control every teenager's behavior and decision-making. Mode of dressing these days, type of music, dance, slang, trends, and even games among the teenagers are now what they learned from social media. You may have noticed this among your friends and classmates.

The most important thing you should focus on now is to identify the kind of difference you will like to make. Not the kind of post you will like to update. If you're not making a difference, then your updates are not making sense.

I felt it necessary to address you one-on-one via a book. I also want to guide you to make sure you're not being carried away by the trends of the virtual lifestyle. At the same time, I will like to help you prepare for future opportunities social media is likely to expose you to. I did not also forget to address the issue of you being watchful of people I call the "social media hunters" who are leveraging social media to commit atrocities most times targeted at innocent teenagers like you.

The social media lifestyle is different from the real-life lifestyle and most of our teenagers are ignorant of this. There are many things they ought to know about social media and I've come to realize that most parents, guardians, counselors, and teachers do not tell most teenagers this... so the knowledge you will learn from this book is vital, remember, life does not pardon people because they're ignorant.

Social media has come to stay...

The internet is here with us and it will stay for so long. Provided we're still using the internet on this planet, then there will always be a place where people gather and interact online.

I wrote this based on the general human behavior on social media and does not deal with the specific functionality of a particular social media platform. That means the principles contained in this book will still be relevant after several years, as long as social media is here with us irrespective of updates, upgrades, new platforms, new apps, changes in codes, and user interface of every social media.

I will advise every home, school, and religious organization to get at least one copy of this book.

Anyone can read it and teach other teenagers the principles contained in it. I believe this will be of great help to you.

MY WORRIES

I specifically wrote this book for African teenagers because I so much believe that the future of this continent is brighter than the present realities.

But we can't go into the next phase of greatness if our today is filled with people who are not conscious of what they're doing. Distracted people can't make a difference.

Image source: dreamstime.com

We're only good at using apps developed by our mates in other continents without thinking of how we can develop ours. At the moment, only a few African digital products are used across the world. The world only knows us as consumers. We don't create.

On a daily basis, many African businesses pay Facebook a huge amount of money for advertisements. You know what that means, we are exporting our wealth to other continents.

I want us to wake up.

Let's not be carried away by trends. There is much more to life than showing yourself on social media. Think of the difference you will make in this life. Anytime you're on social media, think of opportunities. Think of improvements. Think of what you will do to make a difference.

Enough of people in other continents pitying us. We are rich, yet we don't manifest it. But I know if you can get yourself properly aligned and shake off every wave of distractions that filled the air space this time around, then we will change this continent for good.

This generation is waiting for you. We want you to show us what you can do and how you can improve the lives of people across the world. The world is not interested in your clothes and shoes, we're only interested in your latest ideas.

Take your time to read this book. Then set yourself into action.

I want to celebrate you.

NUMBER ONE

WHAT EXACTLY IS SOCIAL MEDIA?

"Keep your heart with all diligence; for out of it are the issues of life"
- Jewish Proverb [a]

Before I give the definition of social media, I will like to drop the words of one of the first-century leaders. He said: *"Do not be misled: "Bad company corrupts good character". [b]*

Let's continue...

Image source: weetracker.com

Definition of Social Media:
According to 'Oxford Languages Dictionary', Social Media are Websites and Applications that enable users to create and share content or to participate in social networking. It is any digital tool that allows users to quickly create and share content with the public.

So, as the name implies, it is used primarily for social interactions in the virtual (online) space.

As social media keeps getting complex by the day, the things they are used for continue to increase. To you as a teenager, this is good news. In another way as well, it could not really mean good news.

Social Media being good or not good in your hands is a function of the discipline you put in using it and also, what exactly you are using it for?

The more the functionalities, features, trends, and modes of interactions on a social media platform increase, the more opportunities it creates for you. At the same time, that's also the more it exposes you to distractions and *"unnecessary noise"*. So discipline and wisdom are very vital as far as social media usage is concerned.

As we can see today across all the social media platforms, they're no more just a place for fun only. It's now a very big environment you can leverage to create any form of advantage for yourself if only you're interested.

The owners of every social media platform keep updating and improving them day by day with new features to suit different people's diversities of interests, preferences, and lifestyles.

So being on social media can never be termed an act of indiscipline or just a waste of time. It's how you use it that's likely to lack discipline on it. If you're disciplined in the use of social media, it will be a great instrument for you as a teenager. If you're a purpose-driven person, you will attract the right people and most times, destiny helpers, via social media.

Maximize The Social Media

As a teenager, that knows what he/she wants from life, and as someone on a journey to becoming a successful and influential adult, what should matter to you most is anything that's adding value to you. If anything you spend your time with doesn't add any value to you, then it isn't really worth the time.

I know social media will help you both in your academics and every other area of your life. It all boils down to your level of discipline, your ability to distinguish values from distractions: your ability to do the right thing at the right time, and also spot and maximize opportunities in them.

A Latin maxim says, *"Tempus fugit non regamus"*. The English translation is: *"time wasted, can never be regained"*. Money wasted can be regained, but you can't regain a wasted time. And I will like to tell you that the greatest asset you have today is time. You have enough time that if you get it right now, you will be a highflyer before many people who are older now. Your time is precious, don't waste it. Use it. Invest it. Maximize it.

USES OF SOCIAL MEDIA

Now, let me show you some of the things that can be done on Social media. I know you're aware of most if not all of them, but let's just run through them and also show you how you can use them to your own advantage:

ONLINE CHATS
This is very common to almost every social media user including teenagers. An average teenager goes on social media to chat with either friends, family members, schoolmates, or maybe, newly met social media friends.

Image source: dreamstime.com

It's very okay to do that... There's absolutely nothing wrong with it. It becomes wrong when the purpose of the chat is likely to hurt you in the future.

Online chats are one of the best, easiest and cheapest ways you can send information as a teenager. If you're on Facebook or WhatsApp and you want to request a note from a classmate and you're short of airtime, then you can simply chat with your close friend who you know is always updated and ask him/her to snap his note or material and send it to you.

So online chats are one of the most major activities people engage on social media and as a teenager who is also a student, you can use them to your own advantage.

Social media chats keep advancing by the day and as at the time of writing this book, voice calls and video calls have been included among the social media chatting methods. This is great and I must tell you, the world has never experienced such before so you're living in the best generation that has ever existed in the history of mankind.

Image source: graphicsmama.com

3 Rules of Social Media Chats You Must Know

Rule #1- You Must Not Reply Every Chats: On your social media account, you will notice that tons of messages will keep coming to you on an hourly basis provided you have a lot of social connections, or maybe, you appear to be very good-looking on your profile photo. That's to say, if you're to go online by 6.00 am and stay there till 6.00 pm, you will be receiving messages non-stop.

Everyone is on social media now. Most people even live there so there will always be someone online to chat with. Don't be carried away.

Most of the people you see online all the time have taken Social media as their home. As a teenager who is going somewhere in the future, you don't want to be like them. If you notice chats that you felt are irrelevant, kindly ignore them. To be on the safe side, don't read it. Some of them might see you as being snobby, but it's self-discipline.

You must not reply to every chat. You see those guys that are always online disturbing you with messages each time you log in, if possible, remove them from your friend list. There's no room to entertain time wasters.

If you've been chatting with someone for at least one week and you can't vividly define what value the person has added to your life within that time frame, then it's time to quit the person.

Rule #2- Chat With Correct English: If you're used to social media abbreviations, then you have to reduce the usage. Chat people with correct English grammar. Don't write *'k'* instead of *'okay'*, don't write *'brb'* instead of *'I will be right back'*, and so on. Make sure your grammar is cool and avoid unnecessary abbreviations.

On this issue of abbreviations, there are some that are obvious people can easily relate to and will like as well but you don't use them in official chats/writings on social media. Some like LOL - lots of laughter, ASAP - as soon as possible, LOML - the love of my life, and so on. But note that these are only used in informal settings.

Rule #3 - Address People by Their Names: If you want to address a person on social media, courtesy demands you do so using their names. For example, instead of just saying *"Hi" to someone, rather* say something like: *"Hi Favor", or "Hello Ken".* A person's name is the best word he can hear in any language. That's why addressing a person by his name will make him engage with you easily because he will see you as someone that values his values.

Why I advise young people to address others this way is because it has a way of passing a positive message about you. You have to be different if you must make a difference.

Let your online chat be awesome. Make your social media chats exceptional and cool. The way you write online reflects the personality you carry in real life.

Image source: 123rf.com

CONTENT SHARING

Another thing you do on social media is content sharing.

Content refers to the different things people write or upload on social media. So anything you see on social media is called *content*.

Content sharing means putting up a post on your social media account for other people's consumption. Content can be texts, graphics, or sound. That means articles, news, pictures, videos, music, infographics, etc, a re all contents.

I know on several occasions you've put up a post on social media. There's nothing absolutely wrong with that. You being courageous to share content means you want your voice to be heard. It can also mean that you're not ashamed of showing the world who you are, what you like, or what you can do.

We need more quality teenage-content-creators in the world today (especially in Africa) and one of the ways you can start is via your own personal social media account.

Image source: mobilise.us

8 Rules of Content Sharing You Must Know

Rule #1- Share Quality and Meaningful Contents:

Your social media posts should be meaningful.
Share quality thoughts and information in your area of interest, skill or talent.

Make your friends, followers, contacts, and connections know who you truly are. Show them what you're made of intellectually and skillfully. This will make them know what they can call you for in case the need arises. Your social media account is your biggest self-promotional tool.

If you truly want to be successful in the future, once you discover your area of gifting, make sure you show it to people connected to you. Promote yourself and your gifts using your social media.

If you love mathematics and dream of becoming a mathematician, a scientist, or an engineer, then talk about mathematics and sciences on your page. If you love literature, discuss literature. If your interest is politics, discuss politics with good and unbiased points.

I'm not saying you shouldn't post "free-style kinds of stuff"; I mean your pictures, your family, friends, and the rest... You're a teenager after all. Make your social media fun and enjoyable but the most important thing is: *Let the majority of your contents show your interest. Let your posts promote you.*

The reason why you should start now in your teenagehood to show your interest or your vision is so people that are connected with you will know when to contact you and what to call you for.

I remember when I was in university in my late teens and early 20s, my social media posts are all motivations because I wanted to be a motivational speaker. That made almost all my friends, coursemates, and colleagues know me as a motivational writer and speaker. So anytime there's a need to give a short motivational talk in any gathering, I'm always the first person that comes to mind...

To date, it has paved the way for me and the foundation of me writing this book can be traced down to it.

Make People Know Your Value... Use Your Social Media Wisely to Promote yourself...

The most important thing you can do for yourself is to make yourself valuable in an area and *let everyone know you for it.*

When people know your value, they will know why they should follow you.

Sharing content on your area of interest will connect you to like minds which will expose you to multiple opportunities. Don't be tempted to do what everyone is doing because you want to be noticed. Do what will attract people that share a similar mindset with you. That's how you can make yourself valuable online.

If you become good at this, then you're on your way to making a fortune in the 21st century way.

Why we have poor adults is because no one knows them for anything.

Image source: theconversation.com

Rule #2- Don't Just Post an Information, Research, and Be Sure Before You Post:
If you're the type that likes posting informational content or breaking news, before you post any of them on social media, make sure you're at least 98.99% sure of it. Don't post based on sentiment, hatred, assumption, or rumor.

Make online searches. Google your facts/information before you throw it out to the public. Believe information only when it's coming from a reliable source.

If your post is misleading, when the real fact is discovered, people will negatively come after you. That's why you need to be sure of whatever content you're dishing out to the public on your timeline. Everyone is posting it doesn't make it true. Post it only if you're sure it is true. On social media beware of crowds.

Try as much as possible to avoid controversial or sentimental discussions.
If you're tempted to join any controversial discussion, do that with wisdom.

Rule #3- Don't Post to Please or Mock Anyone:
I have seen a lot of young teenagers whose posts are targeted at mocking or insulting somebody. That is not good. Anything you do on the internet is public and a lot of people are seeing it. If you're insulting people via your post, then people will start seeing you as someone who likes insults. Desist from posting insulting content.

Image source: freepik.com

If you have issues settling with anyone, don't bring them on social media. If you think you have a friend who is always insulting you in one way or the other, instead of you firing back with a post, why not consider silence or removing the person.

Not keeping malice on social media nor insulting people will give you enough room to focus on yourself and think of how you will become better by the day.

Rule #4- Don't Pretend to Be Who You're Not:

Don't post in order to pretend to be what you are not or claim to have what you don't have yet. I have a lot of teenagers on my Facebook friend list who are pretending to be what they are not. They borrow clothes, shoes, and artificial hairs, pose before a car, etc to snap pictures just because they want to look rich or they want to mock someone or get the person jealous.

They hang around beautiful houses in their neighborhood to snap pictures because they want to pretend to be rich or to come from a rich family… Oh common, don't do that.

Be yourself.

Image source: shutterstock.com

If you have only one cloth… snap pictures with it at different times and different locations and filter the picture. No one will beat you. Be proud of yourself and the level you are at right now.

Neither will anyone slap you. You owe no one anything on social media. None of them is paying you salaries or giving you pocket money so don't try to please or displease anyone. You're only trying to give visibility to your self-image. So, be confident with who you are and be contented with what you have. You are the best for yourself.

Rule #5- Study How People of Similar Interests are Behaving on Social Media:

If you're beginning to think of how you will start sharing your thoughts, ideas, skills, or talent on your social media, I will advise you to start following people that are already doing that and see how they're doing it.

Go on Facebook for instance and search for people that like discussing your topic. Once they come up, follow them and watch how they do their things. Follow them as well on Twitter, LinkedIn, and any other relevant platform. Watch how they post, when they post and how they reply to comments.

That's one of the ways you can start creating a path for yourself towards achieving your dreams.

Rule #6- Don't Write or Structure Your Social Media Posts Like Your Academic Work

When writing content for Internet consumption generally, you don't write it the same you write in your Test, Examination or Academic report. Make it a bit fun. Okay?

Make sure the lines between sentences or paragraphs are properly spaced. That's how you keep them reading and not get tired.

If everything is put in paragraphs of numerous sentences, believe me, only a few fractions of the persons that came across it will read it. But if you space them out and add a little bit of fun to it, then you can engage people and they will keep reading.

Image source: graphicriver.net

Always make use of ellipses, that is "..." at the end of your sentences, and also be using one-sentence paragraphs. If you can develop the skill of drawing people's attention using your social media posts, then you're good.

Rule #7- Use Emojis (Wisely):
The use of emojis is very important. If you're writing content for social media, using emojis on them is very important. Is part of what makes your content engaging. So always include that.

The concept of content creation is very vast and I can't treat it all here. But the insight I've shared with you can take you a long way as a teenager.

If you will like to advance your skill in content creation, then I will advise you to check out some other blog posts online.

Believe me, it's a skill that anyone ought to develop no matter your field of studies or career because, since we are in the internet age, then you should know how to communicate your ideas or expertise to the people on the internet.

CONTENT CONSUMPTION

Another thing people do on social media is content consumption.

Content consumption refers to viewing, listening to, scrolling through, or reading other people's content.

It could be their pictures, their thoughts and opinions, videos, voice posts, and the rest.

It can also be news or updates from newspaper social media pages and brands. In fact, once you're online to see what's going on on your social media apart from chatting, you're actually consuming content.

Image source: time.com

When you visit Facebook, Twitter, or Instagram page of your favorite celebrity or friend to see his/her latest post, what you're doing is *content consumption*. I know on several occasions, what you go online to do is content consumption and not necessarily to chat...

This concept of content consumption is very important because it is the type of content you consume that determines the kind of lifestyle you live. If you keep consuming crappy content, they will have a crappy influence on you. I will advise you, *"don't just be a content consumer, make sure you're also a content creator"*. Create your content and share them on your social media account(s). Write your own article. Do your videos. Share them. Don't hide. Don't be shy. You might not be perfect in it, but whatever it is, put it up and let's see.

My word for you is this: Don't just go online only to read what other people have written. Write your own. Don't just watch other people's videos, think of how you will use your gift to start creating videos for people to see. That gift/talent you have, use it to create content and share on social media. That's why I talked about content creation earlier.

Rules of Content Consumption You Must Know...

Rule - #1: Consume Only Relevant Contents:
Don't be tempted to view or read everything you see on social media.

Some of the social media contents are not created to make you, rather they're created to mar you. That's why you have to be very careful of the people you follow on Twitter and Instagram and people you accept as your friends on your Facebook account.

These days, whenever people want to share immoral and corrupt ideas, they tend to use social media. And you know one funny thing, irrelevant and immoral contents get more engagements and are likely to go viral than the relevant and moral ones.

If any content is not relevant, ignore it. There's no time to waste on irrelevant things. Some social media pages and groups only post nude pictures and videos. Some are specialized in romance and relationships. If these are all that a page or a group can offer to you, then you're wasting your time being there.

Belonging to groups or following pages that are not making you grow are dangerous to your mind and your emotions. The easiest way to hurt yourself is to consume dangerous content. Most people who manage immoral pages/groups don't really have your interest at heart. They only want a massive crowd so they can be selling stuff to them once in a while. Immorality gives good social media engagements, so if any of those fellows want to grow their followers, they start creating immoral content. They don't really want to make an impact or add value, they only want to enrich themselves. Don't be a victim.

As a student, you're supposed to be much busy with things that count. So if you take some time off to be on social media, make that time count. **Social media can be harmful or helpful. It only depends on the kind of content you consume, so be careful.**

You have to discipline yourself in the area of the content you consume. What I mean by this is that you have to put a standard on yourself on the kind of content you will or will not consume.

Till tomorrow, there are popular pages in my country I don't and will not follow. There are popular social media celebrities I can't follow. Once you don't share the same interest or mindset with me, or once I can't learn anything from you on how I will grow, I'm off from you. You too can adopt this kind of style.

This is very important: any content/information you consume gets into your mind. If you consume such information frequently it will sink into your subconscious mind. When it sinks into your subconscious mind, it begins to control your thoughts and your thoughts will always manifest in your behaviors. That's why people who watch a particular comedian's video most times tend to behave like that comedian in real life.

People who keep viewing a particular musician or actor's picture tend to start dressing like him or her. It will get to a point when they start doing this unintentionally.

That's why I'm so much interested in the kind of content you consume. An old Jewish Proverb said, "keep your heart with all diligence..." [a]

So how do you guard your heart as a teenager? Specifically on Social Media...

The simple answer is this: Be careful of the contents you consume on Social Media. Who you follow online tells more about where you're going. I love the social media term, *"follow"*, which means the person is going somewhere and now you're to decide either to join him (follow) or leave him (ignore or unfollow).

Most people/pages do comedy but some of the comedies you see are not good for you as a teenager who is going somewhere.

If you notice a particular comedian who produces comedies that have an immoral undertone, do not hesitate to unfollow such a person. He's not going where you're going.

Peradventure you viewed any of them through a friend's timeline or story, don't view it twice. Keep scrolling dear.

I know you know where you're going already by now, in case you're yet to know, please make out time to discover more of yourself. *If you know where you're going, you automatically know the roads that won't take you there.*

Never allow anyone to contaminate your mind. You're very precious to society.

Contents you consume must either be educating, entertaining (in a positive way), informative, inspiring, motivating, expository and enlightening.

If you notice you just saw content that won't add value to you, kindly ignore it. Don't save it. Don't view it the second time. Just keep scrolling.

In one of the letters of a great first-century leader, he said:
*"Summing it all up, friends, I'd say you'll do best by **filling your minds** and meditating on things true, noble, reputable, authentic, compelling, gracious—the best, not the worst; the beautiful, not the ugly; things to praise, not things to curse"* [c]

So if anything is not true, noble, reputable, authentic, compelling, or gracious, then don't even pay any attention to it.

Rule#2- Don't Get Carried Away:
When I say don't get carried away, I mean don't spend excess time viewing content on social media. I mean, don't give in to wasting your precious time on social media.

When you notice you're beginning to get carried away by social media, retrace your steps and go on with other positive activities you have for the day. Except maybe your time spent there is profiting in the sense that you're studying or marketing a product.

There's something I will like to tell you. It's a secret. The owners of most social media platforms have kept it secret because that's how they make their money. But I will reveal it to you:

Are you aware that the owner(s) of almost every social media platform pay their developers a huge amount of money to make the platform addictive to users? I mean they want to make sure you spend all your time and maybe, your money on the platform.

That's why you keep seeing Facebook, Instagram, YouTube, and the rest adding new features that will keep you engaged on their platform, get you carried away, make you forget your activity for the day, and finally get you addicted. Your being online improves their platforms which ultimately increases their revenue. They want you to sleep there... But you don't want to sleep there.

For instance, when you create a new Facebook account, they will start flashing you with beautiful pictures and the most engaging videos of your new friends or maybe popular pages. They start making multiple friend suggestions to you. Most of the pictures you will be seeing are the ones taken with a high graphics camera.

If you're on Instagram also, once you go search and start to view particular content, Instagram starts flooding you with similar content. Any content they notice much people are viewing, they will start displaying them to you. They don't want you to go leave... they need you there. But you don't want to.

YouTube as well, once you click on a particular video, once that one is ending, YouTube will start showing you other similar videos. Either from the same channel or a different one.

Twitter does similar things. They keep suggesting you follow a particular person who does have higher engagement on his page, maybe a celebrity, because they're looking for a way to keep you staying on their platform and they don't want you to leave.

If you get on Tiktok also, you will keep seeing high engaging video content. They keep flooding your screen often and often. Why? They want you to remain there.

The social media platforms I mentioned here are the popular social media platforms as at the time of writing this book and these are their strategies. I know with time we might have more social media platforms but watch out, they will always use this strategy.
There will always be a tactic to make you love, engage, and get addicted to their platform. Most times it's by flooding you with the most beautiful and most engaging content.

So why are they showing you all these? The answer is this, they don't want you to leave. They want you to remain there and spend all your day there.

My concern is not the money you might be spending. My concern is the time you're likely to be wasting. You can recover the money you're spending on those platforms, but you can't recover the time you've spent there.

By the way, are you aware that the owners of most social media platforms don't spend much time on them?

If you see them online, they're there for a purpose. They're there to do something that will improve the platform. They are there to study the platform, get feedback from most users, and go back and work with their team to improve on it.

Mark Zuckerberg for instance, if you see him make a post on Facebook, know that he's doing that because he wants to tell the world of either his latest achievement, the latest improvement on any of their products or he's about to share his thought on any issue of concern. He hardly posts beautiful pictures of himself. He's not a fashion person or a photo freak. But he owns the world's biggest social media platforms that have turned many into *"fashionistas"* and *"photonics"*.

Image source: fineartamerica.com

Now let's think of it this way as a young teenager who wants to improve himself and become great: if the owners of most social media platform are busy improving themselves and their businesses without minding to constantly post beautiful pictures, count number of likes, comments, shares, or views their posts has gotten, or maybe, constantly checking news feeds to see if the whole world is now on Facebook, then why should you be stressing yourself on it?

If you can get this knowledge right now, you will be the best of yourself in your 20s and many will struggle to consume your content in your 20s. Those who we celebrate today on social media became what they are outside social media. If you have real-life value, then your social media presence begins to make sense.

MARKETING

This is how social media users make money from it and that's also how owners of social media platforms make their money.

I will simply define Marketing for you as the art of promoting your products or services to attract a client. Like I said earlier, this is the aspect where people use social media to make money.

As a teenager, you can leverage your social media network to make money from your friends/followers.

If you have a marketable product, then use your social media accounts to sell them. If you're not selling, you can showcase your parents' own if they're business people. If you don't have any and your parents don't have, and you people have no interest in sales or marketing, then you can forget about it.

Image source: dreamstime.com

If you have a service to render, post it on your social media account.

For instance, If you are very good at mathematics, don't you think that helping people solve their mathematics assignment can be a good business for you?

If you're a very good literature student, then helping your friends/followers solve their literature assignment can be a work for you as well.

There are many lazy students out there who are not willing to sit down and read but are willing to snap their assignments and send them to you to help them solve them. Charge a fee for it, send your account number to them and once you're done with the assignments, snap it and send it back to them.

That's how you can make money from social media.

You see, that's why on content creation, I stressed more on posting things that are relevant and related to your area of interest.

If they know you to be a serious-minded teenager, then they will take you seriously. But if they know you as a social media *"slay queen or slay king"* then anytime you bring up a serious business, they won't listen to you. If people are already seeing you be such on social media, it will take a high level of consistency on serious content for months to change this perception.

Also, apart from just posting products/services on your social media accounts, there's also an advanced form of marketing called *Social Media Marketing*.

If you're a lover of social media, that's how you can use it to make even more money. You can be doing it for yourself or businesses. For instance, when it comes to Social Media marketing there are several things you can do like:

- **Account Management:** This has to do with you being in charge of a social media business page. You post content on it, engage with the fans, respond to inquiries, and also set optimizes it for them.

This is a skill you can develop as a teenager then you can apply to a business to help them manage any of their social media pages while they pay you monthly. It's something you can do with your smartphone and it won't distract you from your academics provided you manage your time well.

- **Content Creation:** This is another work social media can create for you. If you're a good writer or you're good at graphics, you can apply to a Digital Marketing agency to be creating content for them. If you don't know any digital marketing agency, you can use your Google search. Once you apply, tell them you have many wonderful contents they can use to judge your skill and direct them to any of your social media pages. You see why you need to post good and wonderful content in your area of interest.

- **Social Media Advertising:** Social media advertising has to do with you running paid promotions on social media. If you notice very well, each time you're online on any platform at all, you will notice posts from brands that will display on your timeline.

One unique feature about such a post is that it always has something written on it like: "*Sponsored, Promoted, Ad, etc*", while it will have a specific call to action like *Like Page,*

Follow Page, Send Message, Visit Profile, etc, all depending on the platform and the action chosen by the advertiser.

Social Media Marketing is beyond the scope of this book but if you will like to learn more about it, you can check out some resources on it either on Google or YouTube. The reason I will like you to know about social media marketing is that most teenagers across the world are helping themselves through part-time jobs like that and I believe if you pick interest in it you can also use it to support yourself.

You can be working for a digital marketing agency or you can just be on your own and be managing accounts for one or two businesses and they will be paying you depending on your agreement with them.

None of the marketing aspects will distract you from academics because there are tools that will help you automate some of the systems and once you've chosen it as a source of extra income.

If it won't be convenient for you to do any of these depending on your present situation, you can ignore it.

TEACHING
People use social media to teach.

You can find different groups, pages, or people that teach several things across different social media platforms.

No matter what your interest is, you will see a page you will learn something in that area. If you love Physics, look for people that teach Physics and either join their groups or follow their pages. If your interest is Biology or Literature, then look for those pages that teach them and follow.

Whatever you're aspiring to be has a group on social media. Be it a medical doctor, a lawyer, banker, etc, you will always find the group on social media. I will advise you to find one and join. Watch how they do things and learn from them. If you have questions to ask, feel free to do so on the group.

Groups like that will expose you to diverse knowledge and help you connect with people you can get relevant information from.

Once you're in any group, have it in mind also that most people are there for different purposes. So be careful about who you become close to. Your purpose should be defined. You're there to gain knowledge and exposure in your area of interest, so anything aside that should be ignored.

Your presence on social media as a teenager must profit yourself and not just to 'pass time'.

Also, there are special groups/pages that teach a particular subject. For instance, some groups have in them mathematics lovers who on a daily basis, post mathematics questions, and have you crack your brain to solve them. You will see other teenagers like you solving these questions and bringing out their ideas in the comment section.

Recently, I've learnt a lot of Mathematics tricks from some guys on Tiktok. There are many guys on that App that specialises on teaching mathematics tricks which can help you become fast in solving mathematics and also pass external examinations.They have a good following across the world and most of them are Africans. You too can learn from them.

That's so interesting… You can be part of it as well.

NETWORKING
Networking has to do with meeting and interacting with new people. Networking is also more of finding people who are interested in your interest. It doesn't necessarily mean making new friends. It

means meeting people who are going where you are going or people who are already where you want to be.

This is one of the biggest roles social media is meant to play for you as a teenager. You meet people who have the same vision, goal, and purpose as you. Not people who want you to spend the whole weekend chatting with you about a TV concert or your favorite artist.

Why I keep stressing about having people who are interested in your interest is that most social media users and just there to hunt for young teenagers like you. ***Once you notice anyone is not making sense, BLOCK the person.***

Another important thing I will like to tell you on networking is this, once you meet any new person, or join any new group or follow any new page and you're constantly in touch with either the person, the group, or the page, please kindly let your parents know about it. Show them and let them tell you what they think about the page, the group the person.

If someone you don't know is constantly messaging you, don't hesitate to show your parents. ***Let Your Parents Know Everything You Do On Social Media.***

CONCLUSION:
The essence of this chapter is to make sure you make the best use of your social media account.

My concern is to make sure you're online to learn and grow and not to waste your time.

All these I outlined are what you can use your social media account for. Social media is meant for wasting time. It's for adding values.

If your social media is not adding any value to you, then you're just wasting your time and your money.

NUMBER TWO

HOW TO BECOME A TEENAGE SOCIAL MEDIA INFLUENCER

"if you want something you have never had, you must be willing to do something you have never done"
– Thomas Jefferson

In every environment, some people make things happen. They set the pace and others follow. Once there is a trend in the social media space, it will always be linked to them. They create it... their followers spread it... So who are they? The correct word we can use for them is **Leaders**. That's why leadership was defined by John C. Maxwell as influence, nothing more, nothing less. [a]

In this chapter, we are going to talk about people who are leaders in the social media space.

If you're used to social media especially platforms like Twitter and Instagram, you will always hear people use the word *influencer*. Each time anything happens on social media they attribute it to Influencers.

But I will like to ask this question: **Who is a Social Media Influencer**?

A social media influencer is a person who has the ability or capacity to affect the way people think or react to an event using social media.
They can affect peoples' decisions and choices across a particular social media platform. They are highly respected on social media and that also gains them real-life respect and influence.

Social media influencers are known to have a massive number of followers and every of their post always have good engagements and interactions. in order words, they are famous. Anything they post online people believe it and act according to their instructions. If they introduce a hashtag or a challenge, people will always join and make it go viral.

Social media users always respect influencers and that's why most businesses use them to advertise their products on social media because they believe that users of the platform will always believe what they say.

If you're an influencer, you automatically become a celebrity and once you're a celebrity, you automatically become an influencer. A celebrity is someone the majority of the people celebrate and once many people celebrate you, you can influence them.

It is good to be an influencer. That's what everyone is dreaming to become. No one wants to be a nobody. Everyone wants to have a voice.

So the question is this: **How Do You Become a Social Media Influencer Even As a Teenager?** Let me show you five ways you can become a social media influencer as a teenager and they're as follows:

1.BE THE BEST OF WHO YOU ARE
"do you see a man skilled in his work? He will serve before kings; he will not serve before ordinary men" [b]
– Jewish Proverb

The proverb above just explained to us that what you need to stand out from the crowd is to get exceptionally skilled in your work. If you are not such, then never expect to stand out. Everyone is doing the same thing, so if you want to stand out, you need to become exceptionally different.

I have seen a lot of teenagers who try to do wrong things just because they want many followers or maybe, they want many people to like their photos, watch their videos, or share their contents. Some teenagers try to show themselves half naked on social media because they believe that's what they have to do to draw people's attention to themselves. They join irrelevant trends and post immoralities because they're looking for massive followers on social media. These are wrong. Anyone doing such is simply creating problems for himself because anything you post on the internet will always remain there.

Some teenagers borrow jewelry, expensive clothes, and expensive gadgets including snapping in an expensive house that doesn't belong to their parents just because they feel that's how to become a celebrity. I'm not saying looking nice on your social media photos are wrong, I only don't want you to feel comfortable and proud with what you have at the moment and shake yourself off the pressure of trying to feel "belong".

It's the desire to appear as a celebrity on social media and subsequently an influencer, that young people are joining internet fraud because they want to show off money, wine, gadgets, and "Benz".

Each time I see young people behave in this manner, my heart bleeds, because they are doing the wrong thing and at the same time, dangerously harming their future.

Anyway, I don't blame people for behaving in such a manner. Going by what you see every day on social media, no one talks of diligence and hard work. No one is encouraging the younger generation anymore to focus on studies, build their potentials and live a fulfilled life. Everyone is busy showing an easy kind of lifestyle with free and quick money. Most of our celebrities don't show us behind the scenes the efforts that made them who they are. They're only showing the glory they have presently without minding to show the world the real story. And this is why teenagers think that's how a celebrity should be so they end up doing things the wrong way.

Celebrities took their time to build their dreams and potentials including mastering their talents. It is not by showing off on the internet, so sit down and focus on building yourself.

Now let me tell you this: You don't force yourself to become a celebrity, you work yourself into it. You don't force yourself to become influential, you earn it through diligence, discipline, and consistency.

This is something you should always remember: *"Good Success Makes You Influential."*

It means once you're successful in one area of life, you automatically become influential in areas of life.

This is why a star musician in your country will say something about politics and many people will agree with him because he's successful in music. An actor can make you like a particular clothing brand, why? because he or she is successful in movies.

In Nigeria for instance, Chimamanda Adichie can make people change their opinion about a particular societal issue because she's successful in literature. Elon Musk can make people change their investment decisions because he's a successful man.

Hence, once you're successful in one area of life, you automatically become influential in almost every area of life. Success brings you influence.

So if success is what makes you influential, then you're not meant to struggle to become influential, you're only meant to focus on becoming successful. That's why your greatest focus now should be on how to make yourself better and not how to make people like you. Success is not what you pursue, it is what you become by obeying some laws.

Once you're successful, people have no choice but to follow you and hear your story. If you want me to follow you, I must be able to define what I will benefit from you before I follow you.

If you can't make me better, then don't expect me to follow you. So, focus on yourself first. Become good at something then tell us what it is, we will then follow you and engage with your content.

Successful people are naturally attractive. So if you want to attract, then become successful.

How To Become Successful
"if you want to be successful, do not seek success. Seek to become a person of value"
– Myles Munroe

A successful first-century leader once told his teenage mentee, *"study to show that you're worthy to be accepted by the people..." [c].* In those words he meant; you know there are people out there who are older than you, or who might even be more learned than you. But if you must be worthy to get their attention, then you need to study diligently.

Image source: 123rf.com

That means you need to make yourself valuable before people would accept you.

Your success as a teenager depends on how valuable you are in anything you're doing. Being valuable in a thing means you're skilled in it.

So what will make a huge number of persons to follow you on social media is how much you can deliver value to them. Not how much you can disturb them with your pictures of rice and beans.

I repeat this once more, *Make yourself valuable, then People will follow you.*

It is the quality and the value of the content you share that determines whether you will become a social media influencer or not.

Why…? People only follow those with value. Don't be a social media noisemaker, be a social media newsmaker. Newsmakers give value and people struggle to get in touch with them for their values. Noisemakers only drop empty words with no value while the purpose is attention-seeking.

Don't even try to attract people, No. Don't force people to view your post, comment, or like. No. Give them a value, then they have no option other than to engage with you. Once your contents have value, people will share it and hence, more engagement and followers.

For instance, imagine you're good at summarising literature novels you read in your classes and you put it on social media. Believe me, anyone that's reading the same novel will like to connect with you, share your posts, and get other of his friends and mates to connect with you. That's how you become attractive.

Also, assuming you're good in mathematics. And you're always giving highlights of some topics on your page depending on the academic curriculum for the term, now look, all students who love mathematics and those who want to be good in mathematic will like to connect with you, no matter the platform you're using. They will like to see how you're solving it and will be willing to learn from you. That's how you can grow a good network of mathematics lovers.

Let me talk about skills…

If you're good at hairdressing or catering, you can always post your skills on your social media wall. You can also teach how you manage to do those wonderful things. People who have an interest in such will start following you to learn and to identify with you. They're also likely to recommend clients to you. By so doing, you're building a network of the lovers of your skill and potential clients. That's one of the best and easiest ways you can monetize your skill as a teenager.

Before you know it, you will discover that your followers are increasing and from there, you become an influencer.

Stop stressing yourself trying to make people like and follow you.

Go and master a skill.

Go and master at least one subject.

Make yourself valuable first... Then people will follow you because they know they will gain something from you.

That time you're using to check how many people have liked your picture or followed your page, use it to work on yourself.

When you're valuable, you're attractive... and when you're attractive, you're successful, and when you're successful you're influential.

2. BELONG TO A MAXIMUM OF TWO PLATFORMS

As a student, you need to be very careful about how much time you spend on social media. That is why belonging to multiple social media platforms can be of great disadvantage to you. Belonging to multiple social media platforms is nothing but a distraction.

Select just two platforms and belong there and be sharing your content there. This will help you manage your time very well, make you a social media person and still keep you focused on your academics.

Check the ones that will work best for you and register there. You can leave every other one.

Imagine only you, a student, you're on Facebook, Instagram, Twitter, Snapchat, Tik-Tok, Likee, WhatsApp together with a YouTube channel... Hmmm... That's too much for you man. Except you have someone helping in managing them, but if you're the only one managing your account, limit yourself to only two.

You must not belong to all social media platforms. Curtail your distractions by belonging to a maximum of two and stay focused on them. In the future, you can expand your social media networks but now is not necessary for you.

One good thing with belonging to a maximum of two is this if you're able to gather many fans on the two you've focused on for years, the day you will want to create an account on another platform, it will be very easy for you to amass followers. All you need do is announce on your page that you just created an account on another social media platform and you will see how your fans who also belong to that platform will rush and follow you.

Once you're a person of value, you're needed everywhere.

3. THINK OF WRITING A BOOK
I know this might sound somehow but it's a good idea I want to reveal to you. That your gift you always talk about, you can write a book on it and publish it. If you can achieve this as a teenager, then know that your worth, your level, and your influence will so much increase. Once you do it and publicize it on your handle, you will begin to attract respect.

I know you might be thinking that it's a big deal to publish a book, but I want to tell you that is not. Thanks to Amazon Kindle Direct Publishing (KDP). It has simplified the process and I will like you to utilize it. It allows you to submit your manuscript to Amazon and they will do the printing and publishing for you. It's called Print on Demand so you don't have to spend thousands to publish it and pack it in your house. Amazon does the whole thing for you.

But, If you don't want to produce a physical book as that might involve extra work on you, you can produce an ebook. Just type your book on your computer system and save it as a PDF document, then you've produced an ebook.

Once you produce a book, publicize it online. If it's an ebook, you can consider selling it at a very cheap price or you simply give it out for free. I want you to produce a book at most in the next one year after reading this book.

If you like hairdressing, write a book on hairdressing. If you like Mathematics, write a book on how you fall in love with mathematics and your secrets to understanding and solving it without stress. If you're gifted in singing, then write a book on how to become a teenage singer.

You don't need to struggle to think about what you will write about. Your personal story alone is a book, so think of writing a book. Once you've conceived an idea on the topic you will be writing about, seek help and advice from people older and more experienced than you on how to about other things. You can relate to your parents or a close teacher and see how they will help you bring this dream into a reality.

Write a book... Your influence will grow. When you write your book, get across to me I will buy one from you.

4. KEEP PROMOTING YOURSELF
Once you're making yourself valuable, be promoting yourself. Tell your siblings to promote you. If you don't have an elderly sibling, then mum and dad should always be doing that. They should keep showing the world the progress you're making. Always tell mum and dad to celebrate you on social media.

It is very important to let your parents know of anything you're doing including your social media activities. Don't keep them in the dark. If you're doing great in your subjects, mum and dad should celebrate with you. If you're learning a new skill and you're getting good at it, share your knowledge and experience with them and ask them to help in promoting you on their social media accounts.

All these are what will increase your influence as a teenager and prepare you for a glorious future. I want to see you at the top.

STORIES OF SOME INFLUENCERS

I have been on social media since 2006 when I was in my second year in junior secondary school and I must tell you that I've experienced lots of stories of people who became influencers through their personal success stories.

Just one success story can make you influential and you gather a massive following across your social media channels. I have some of them below:

1. Influencer Through Academic Achievement

Chike was a sixteen-year-old teenager who just concluded secondary school in Owerri, Imo state Nigeria and wrote his West African Secondary School Certificate Examination (WASSCE). The same year he wrote the University Tertiary Matriculations Examination (UTME).

Fortunately, Chike made straight As in the nine (9) subjects he wrote in WAEC. When his Tertiary Matriculations Examination result came out, he scored 346/400 making him the highest in the state.

With this euphoria and excitement, Chike took to his Twitter account to announce and celebrate his outstanding success in both examinations. In less than 48 hours, his followers on Twitter grew and he suddenly became influential because many other teenagers were willing to listen to him, read his post, and see how he was able to make such an outstanding success.

I will like you to share this kind of story. So focus and read your books. Success will always make you influential.

2. Influencer Through an Outstanding Skill

In 2019, a car manufacturing company in Nigeria called for a Logo design contest on Twitter. They asked graphics designers to design a new and beautiful logo for the company. Different graphics designers joined the contest by designing a logo for this company and shared them on social media.

Finally, a very young man by the name Farooq won the contest and the company decided to announce him on their Twitter handle together with his Twitter username. Immediately they tweeted him as the winner, the young man started gathering massive followers. It also gave him more contracts. People then wanted to know how come he's good in graphics in such a manner that made him win such a great national contest. Many were also willing to sign up and get trained by him for any amount.

How come all these were coming because he is successful.

3. Becoming a DJ from Age 8 Made Her Influential

DJ Switch Ghana is a young girl from Ghana who became influential due to her love for music and her Disc Jockey (DJ) skill.

She has won several awards in her country and across the world, because she mastered the skill of being a DJ. I've seen her perform music on stage with Wyclef Jean in the US and she has appeared on several international billboards.

She's been featured on several media outfits including BBC, and several radio and TV stations across Africa.

Image source: techprevue.com

It is her mastery of DJ skills that made her an influence. She is the first Ghanian DJ to get 100k subscribers on YouTube and it has continued to increase. She has a massive following on Instagram. One good thing about her is that she's a good reader, doing very well in her academics, and also creates quality time at home to practice and master her DJ skills.

As at the time of writing this book, her social media account is being managed by her mother because she's still too young while she focuses more on herself.

You can learn from her.

4.Running Successful Startup Made Them Influential

Two young Nigerians Shola Akinlade and Ezra Olubi founded a startup in 2015 which is a payment gateway they named Paystack. They ran this startup successfully for 5 years and were able to attract several investors across the world to invest in the startup. In the year 2020, another bigger company from the United States by the name Stripe bought this business for $200 million.

Immediately the news broke out on the Internet, it started trending on social media across Nigeria and what was going on in everybody's mind is Who are the founders of Paystack?

This made their social media followers grow and their influence grew as well.

Being successful in running a startup in Nigeria made them popular and influential.

CONCLUSION

When you're valuable you become successful, and success gives you influence.
What you should seek is how to make yourself better today than how you were yesterday.

You make yourself valuable based on your daily activities. If you're committed to a particular course diligently, then the result will be a success.

Pay attention to your books. Be a master in your skill.

Master at least one academic subject and show the world that you're good at it. If you're already in a tertiary institution, thank God for that. Show us what's happening around the world regarding the course you're studying. Doing this alone on LinkedIn will expose you to great opportunities both now you're in school and after school.

If you make yourself valuable, then the world will follow you. That's how you become influential.

Keep developing yourself and let your friends and family help in promoting you. You are a STAR.

NUMBER THREE

HOW TO CULTIVATE A GOOD SOCIAL MEDIA SELF-ESTEEM

"as a man thinks in his heart, so is he..." [a]
– Jewish Proverb

"We all know that self-esteem comes from what you think of yourself, not what other people think of you" **- Gloria Gaynor-**

It will be very vital I address the issue of self-esteem. Your self-esteem has a lot to do with the quality of life you live. When your self-esteem is not sound, then you will not have a sound lifestyle. What makes you confident or timid anywhere you are is a result of your self-esteem.

Studies have shown that social media is fuelling low-self esteem among young people. I don't want you to fall this victim. Your self esteem should not be a product of what you see from social media.

Image source: 123rf.com

I want you to live a healthy lifestyle with a sound mind as you use your social media. if you get the concept of self-esteem right, you will be very great in life.

I brought this topic into this book because I have seen a lot of people who suffer inferiority complex and most times depression as a result of what they saw on social media. Most of them after visiting platforms like Instagram, get depressed thinking that their mates are doing better than them. I want you to cancel such a mindset.

You need to get this concept right so you get depressed when you see updates from other people.

So let's dive in...

What is Self Esteem?

Self-esteem means how you feel or what you think about yourself.

3 TYPES OF SELF-ESTEEM

The 3 types of self-esteem we have are:

1. Inflated Self-Esteem: People with inflated self-esteem think they are better than others and have no doubts about underestimating everyone else. This is very negative self-esteem, as it holds them back from establishing affectionate and healthy relationships.

2. Low Self-Esteem: This is negative self-esteem. People with low self-esteem **do not value themselves, they do not trust in their possibilities.** Fear of failure is something that torments people with low self-esteem and holds them back. They feel bad about themselves and always think they are not good enough. They are the model of unhappy people.

3. High Self-Esteem: This will be our main focus in this chapter. People with this kind of self-esteem **accept and value themselves.** It is self-esteem that is known to be positive and good, as it manages to make the person satisfied with their life.

Believing in yourself and trusting in who you are is what characterizes people who possess this type of self-esteem. This is the kind of self-esteem I want you to develop and have.

"Persons of high self-esteem are not driven to make themselves superior to others; they do not seek to prove their value by measuring themselves against a comparative standard. Their joy is being who they are, not in being better than someone else" **-Nathaniel Branden-**

HOW YOU CAN BUILD A HIGH SELF-ESTEEM

1. Be With People Who Treat You Well: This applies to both online and offline. Some people act in ways that tear you down. Others lift you by what they say and do. *Learn to tell the difference.* Choose friends who help you feel okay about yourself. On social media, follow people who write words that lift you up and not those who make gest of people who they feel they're better than.

Also, find people you can be yourself with. Be that type of friend for others. On your social media, never should you be the kind of person that thinks you're better than others. Always write words that speak good of the people that are following.

2. Ignore Negative Comments: I have come to understand that no matter how good you try to become, there will always be someone who is not happy with you. That's why no matter how good, educating, or inspiring a YouTube video is, there will always be someone who will click the "dislike" button on it. Everyone must not like you. Everyone must not agree with you. It's a normal thing about life.

If people are always dropping negative comments on your articles, pictures, or videos, just allow them. It's normal. What you only need to do is to ignore them.

What anyone thinks about you is not necessary. The necessary is what you think about yourself.

MY FINAL WORDS FOR YOU

It is harmful to think less of yourself. It is dangerous to be on Social Media with low or Inflated Self-esteem.

The worst thing that can happen to you as a teenager is to think less of yourself and depend on other peoples' approval to feel better about yourself.

In case you don't know, the value you place on yourself is much better than the value others place on you. What people think about you doesn't matter at all. What matters is what you think about yourself.

I once read a story of a fourteen-year-old girl in America who committed suicide for two main reasons: One is that she's having poor likes on Instagram photos and the second is that people are always commenting on her photo that she's ugly.

So because of this, she killed herself. That what low self-esteem can lead to.

Most teenagers exhibit questionable attitudes on social media because they want to feel involved.

They believe by such, people will accept them. But that's wrong.

How To Develop a Good Self Esteem

Self-esteem is a product of the mind. What you think you are is what you are. No one is ugly. Is just people's thought about a person. Also, you're not ugly. The problem is you think you're ugly.

If you must develop good self-esteem, there's something you must have in mind and that is this: you're the best person on earth and anywhere you are, you're important there and you are needed.

Be yourself.

Image source: lifehack.org

That's why I talked about focusing on developing your skill or your academic prowess in other to become successful. If you're developing your skills and reading your books, never feel less in any company at all.

On social media, you're the most beautiful person there. Whether anyone likes your picture or not, the truth is you like the picture. Once you update anything online, **be the first to LIKE it.**

A first-century leader once wrote a letter to his teenage mentee. In one of the letters, he made a statement that is very important that every teenager including yourself must know.

He said; *"...let no man look down on you because you are young... but always show good examples in your conversations and way of thinking. Till I be with you again, make sure you give proper attention to essential knowledge from vital sources..."*

So he was telling him not to allow anyone to look down on him on any grounds at all, be it because of age or any other classification.

In other words, he's letting him know that being a teenager doesn't mean he doesn't have a voice. He also meant no matter what or who you are at the moment, that should not be a reason why anyone should look down on you. He further told him to pay attention only to self-development and never consider people looking down on him as a limiting factor.

Those statements were made for him to strengthen up his self-esteem and feel comfortable with any company no matter the people involved. No matter the kind of friends you have on Facebook or the kind of followers you have on Instagram, none of them should look down on you for any reason.

Allow people with their own opinion, but never accept it to be true of yourself. You're the most handsome and the most beautiful. Your intelligence can never be compared with any and believe me, you're getting much better every day.

If you have poor self-esteem, then you can't become valuable on social media. And if you're not valuable, then you can't be influential. I have never seen a rich man with low self-esteem. Once you have good self-esteem, you will become successful.

People will always see you how you see yourself.

If you see yourself as someone not fit to be seen or heard by many, then people will see you the same way. But if you're always bold and confident of yourself, then people have no option but to be under your influence.

Have this consciousness that you're a global star and the whole is expecting to see and hear you. No matter how your face is. No matter the color of your teeth. No matter the size of your nose or the shape of your legs, those things do not matter.

I know of a Ghanian social media celebrity called "Shatta-Bandle". To most people, he's not that a very "good-looking" young man. But to himself, he the most handsome, intelligent, and richest man on social media. He's full of confidence not minding what you're thinking about him. And that has made him popular, valuable in the entertainment industry, and rich as well. In case you don't know him, please Google to see his picture.

The most important thing here is that you have a value capable of impacting lives across the world. Don't see yourself as a child. Young people are the ones making things happen now. If you see yourself as a child then you're denying yourself of being heard by society.

I have come to realize that these days, once a teenager does something outstanding, it goes viral and gains recognition more than when a fully grown adult does the same thing. Most people will like to see the little Dj Switch Ghana perform at their wedding or birthday ceremony than seen a 35-year-old DJ.

Anything you are, feel comfortable to show it. Anything you know, feel comfortable to teach the world. Have good self-esteem.

You're a child of success.

NUMBER FOUR

4 NEGATIVE SOCIAL MEDIA INFLUENCE YOU SHOULD AVOID

"Everything is permissible for me, but not everything is beneficial. Everything is permissible for me, but I will not be mastered by anything" [a]
– Paul (A First Century Leader)

It is good to use social media media, but don't let social media use you. It is good to control a smartphone, but don't let a smartphone control you.

It is good to use the Internet, but don't let the Internet use you. From the quote written in the introduction, the writer realized that there are things that are okay for him to do but such things will not control him.

You need to be watchful of some negative influence of social media so you don't end up a victim of any. Social media is meant for you, you are not meant for social media so you must be careful of being influenced by it negatively.

Some of the effects are as follows:

Image source: wsj.com

1. SOCIAL MEDIA ADDICTION

Most teenagers today are becoming addicted to social media. Their daily lives and activities are built around social media that they spend even their productive hours checking for updates and notifications on their social media accounts. I want to believe you're not one of them.

How will you wake up in the morning and the first thing you do is to visit your social media accounts? Do you go to check if your last picture update has generated 1M engagements? Or do you want to know if truly you're topping your friends in terms of likes and comments? No dear, that's very wrong.

Never start your day with social media.

How will you be in school and immediately a teacher/lecturer is done with the class the next thing you do is to bring out your smartphone to check your social media? Oh… That's very wrong also. When you see yourself behaving that way, then know you're becoming addicted to social media.

Don't be on social media during your productive hours of the day. Except on special occasions when it becomes necessary maybe because it's your source of information, then go ahead. But if it's just for leisure, don't do that. Instead, go on the Internet and look for topics related to what you're studying and read about them.

Facebook should not replace your book. Social media activities should not substitute your studies. Social media addiction is something you should try as much as possible to avoid.

If you discover you're already addicted to social media, believe me, you can still overcome it. It's a habit you've built and believed me, habits can be unlearned.

How to Avoid Social Media Addiction

I. Have a Vision For Your Life: A Jewish proverb says: *"where there is no vision, people lose self-control..."* [b]. You see, what most times make people behave anyhow is lack of vision for one's life: people not knowing where they are going in life and what they truly want from life.

If you can't define where you're going, that's when you can easily be carried away by any form of distractions including social media. A man of vision already knows his destination and can hardly get addicted to what will not let him get there. That's why I mentioned earlier that you should work on developing your gifts, talents, and abilities first. Self-discovery leads to self-control.

Social media should not come first. Your life vision should come first.

Can being on social media all through the weekend make you pass your exams? The answer is NO. Can being on social media all through the night make you master the skill of being a programmer? The answer is NO. That's why I'm advising you to first have a vision for your life.

If you want to be a medical doctor, then social media should be the last thing you think of. Your science subjects come first. Your calculations and your practicals take the most priority. Social media should be the last in your mind. Most of my medical doctor friends are not active on social media and they owe no one an apology for that. Their life's purpose has kept them so busy that they have no time for distractions anymore.

So if you're a teenager with a vision, then working on yourself becomes your ultimate goal.

I know some of your friends might criticize you for not being active on social media, but that shouldn't bother you. When you actualize that vision you're pursuing and you chose to showcase yourself using your social media account, believe me, you will gain more traction than them. That attention and fame they're trying to gain by wasting their time on social media, you will get them cheaply if you achieve your life vision.

Now, what do you want from life?
Write it down on paper and paste it on the wall in your room. Look at it every morning when you wake up.
Each time you notice you're beginning to waste much time on social media, look at it and ask yourself, can staying 5 hours on Facebook chatting with my friends make me become this that I want to be in the future?

If your answer is NO, then close that app and start doing what's necessary. One of the leaders that lived in the first century told some of his followers that: *"there are lots of things to be done which are good, but not all of them are necessary"* [c].

So, if social media is not necessary for your vision, then stop spending so much time on it

II. Master The Art Of Time Management: Time management is a skill you must master. Learn how to utilize your time to your utmost benefit and pursuit of purpose. If you're conscious of your time, you will be careful about how you use it.

Everyone has 24 hours in a day., nature did not give anyone extra. But how everyone uses theirs differs. How you use your time and what you use it on is what determines whether you will be a success or a failure. That is why time management is very important.

Don't start your day with social media. If you start

your day with social media you're likely to ruin your whole day and your 24 hours will not be properly utilized. Why did I say this: Imagine you just woke up from bed and you went straight to Instagram, all of a sudden you see the news of the death of your favorite actor/actress. The truth is that if you should start your day like this, then your day is completely ruined already.

Same way, don't end your day with social media.

Anything that will make you not use your time well, avoid it. Remember, time waits for no one. Use it wisely.

One of the most vital ways to manage your time is to plan. Once you wake up every morning, depending on your religious belief, you say your prayer. After that, then go on and pick your jotter/diary and write down everything you wish to achieve that day.

When you're leaving your house for school, make sure you keep an eye on it. Once you actualize any, mark it done.

That way, you can track your progress, and make you not waste your time unnecessarily.

If you want to go on social media any day, write down how long you will spend there. Remember I told you earlier that the owners of social media are constantly building it to make it addictive to you. So don't be a victim.

No matter the flashy updates, the engaging videos, and the interesting chats you're receiving, if you plan to stay on Instagram for 45 minutes, once that time elapses, close the App.

The developers of social media keep making it that there's always something to keep you engaged on social media. So don't be carried away when you start seeing them. That's how the platform is designed. It's designed to get you addicted to them so they will keep making more money out of your engagement.

I told you earlier that the owners of these social media platforms don't spend much time using them. Rather they spend much time researching how to make them better. Even their employees spend less time on them. They're always busy working on how to make them better.

I want to tell you also, don't spend much time on them. Rather spend much time on making yourself better.

III. Install Freezing Apps: Some applications can help you manage the use of other applications. These apps are very necessary because they help you manage how you use the other applications thereby making you not get addicted to any of them nor waste much time on them. What these apps do is make some distracting applications inactive for a while until you reactivate them. *I don't mean unistall here.*

If you're someone that can easily get distracted by social media notifications, maybe once you see a notification you go to check what's that or who is that, then you need to be freezing some of your social media applications. That will keep you focused so you do the necessary things on your Smartphone.

I do that myself. There are times when all my social media Apps will be inactive except for a very vital one. It helps me checkmate my excesses and that has helped me from being a victim of social media addiction.

So you can do the same. Don't let those notifications make you go online when is not yet time. Search for those Apps from the App-Store of your mobile operating system and install them.

2. ERRONEOUS BELIEFS

Another thing social media has done excellently is making young people develop some erroneous beliefs. Some errors are developed by some people and they use social media to propagate them. Be careful not to fall victim to it.

These beliefs vary according to different countries but check in your country, some people are bringing up controversial and dangerous beliefs and they are spreading it using social media, once you spot any of them, keep scrolling and avoid them.

Most people have used social media to propagate teaching that criticizes different religions. So have used social media to tarnish other people's images and make people develop a wrong perception about them. Kindly desist from such.

Once you notice any teaching or philosophy making rounds on social media, trying to counter an already existing belief before you adhere to it, seek counsel from your parents, teachers, guardian, or your religious leader. In this case, your mind is secured.

There are agents of erroneous beliefs who are using social media to sell their errors. Be watchful of them.

Mind who you listen to on social media. Most of them are out to pollute your heart.

How To Avoid Erroneous Beliefs
I. Avoid listening to or following controversial persons. There are many people the majority of the people see to have controversial beliefs. To be on the safe side, don't follow or listen to them.

II. Always seek your parents' counsel on anything you learn from social media. Feel free to relate to them. Don't just learn without asking for your parents' opinions. Hear their opinion. I'm not talking about knowledge that has to do with your school subjects. I mean teaching that propagates a belief, maybe about family, business, relationships, money, life, religion, name it. Once you hear such, don't just digest it on your own, share it with your parents.

III. Have a Mentor: A mentor is someone who guides you and is committed to helping you see you actualize your vision. A mentor knows what's right and what's wrong for you. If you have a mentor, that means anytime you gain any form of knowledge, you simply relate to him or her and that

3. WRONG PERCEPTION
Social media can instill in you the perceptions. There is stuff which in real life might seem to be abnormal but social media portrays them to be normal. For instance, Social Media often portrays grown-ups to be cool if they eat junk food, smoke, drink alcohol, use drugs, drive fast, etc. All these presentations of adult life can influence you. Most times, making you emulate your favorite celebrities/influencers in the wrong way.

How To Avoid the Wrong Perception From Social Media
I. Know that Social Media Life is different from real life. So don't let people's social media lifestyle make you think that's how real life is. Don't try to live the lifestyle you saw on social media in real life. Both are different.

II. If social media doesn't benefit you, kindly avoid it. Being on Social Media is not compulsory, It's just a matter of choice. If you think what you're seeing here is not really for you, you can quit it. It's not a criterion for being successful. But if you're okay, then go on but follow my advice.

CONCLUSION
I always maintain the position that one of the major things you need to be successful is discipline. If you're not disciplined in each of your daily activities you will not get good results.

Also, spot when you're being influenced negatively by social media. I know your family has a standard they're setting for you. If you begin to see anything on the contrary via your social media please don't hesitate to inform either your parents or your guardians.

If you're being pressurized in any way or by anyone on social media, make your parents know about it.
See You At The Top.

NUMBER FIVE

5 WAYS TO APPEAR RESPONSIBLE ON SOCIAL MEDIA

"The beginning of wisdom is this: Get wisdom. Though it cost all you have, get understanding." *[a]* -**Jewish Proverb**

Your social media account is like your house online. How your house is is a description of how you are. When people who have not meant you in person want to know the kind of person you are, they simply visit your social media profile to see the kind of person you are. Hence, there is a need to make your social media account look responsible.

How responsible you appear on social media is what will determine how people will chat you up and the kind of persons that will be attracted to you. If you appear responsible then you will attract responsible people. If you appear irresponsible then irresponsible persons will be attracted to you.

There's this popular saying that how you dress is how you're addressed. In the same way, the way how you appear on social media is the way people will approach you. If you're a girl for instance, and you notice that boys are always sending the wrong type of messages to you. It's simply because you presented yourself as someone they can have anyhow. The kind of messages you receive is a reflection of the personality you portray on your social media account.

If you present yourself as a responsible person, believe me, people will approach you on your DM and comment session responsibly.

How you appear is how you're approached.

So, How do you appear responsible?

1. Use Your Real Name (Except You're Promoting Your Personal Brand)

You as a teenager should answer your real name on social media. Don't be fake. Be real. *If your name is Amaka Koffi, write it. Don't use Itz Mak-Kofi Baby.*

I repeat, use your real name. If anyone sees you answering your real name on social media, it gives the impression that you know who you truly are, you're proud of yourself and you're confident of who you are.

Using your real name will make people respect you and will be willing to discuss something meaningful with you because they can see you're real and you're a serious person. Imagine answering a funny name and you come out to teach your social media followers or friends about the recent study you made in your biology subject over the week. Most of them won't even take you seriously because you didn't appear serious.

So if you want to start now to touch lives in your little sphere, use your real name on social media.

But I want to put a clear and decent exemption.

If you already have a personal brand, I mean if as a teenager you're already into something like fashion, music, DJ, blogger, or any other form of performance and people know with a particular name because of what you're doing already, in this case, you can choose to be answering that name.

For instance, if you're into music and you play with saxophone and people already know you as Prince Sax, in this case, you can answer that on social media to make it easier for people who already know you with that stage name to connect with you. But if it's not something similar to that, please use your real name.

You're aspiring to be a medical doctor, lawyer, politician, pharmacist, engineer, military, or para-military personnel, use your real name.

Present yourself to be a responsible person then the people will take you seriously.

2. Use a Descent Profile Picture:
Your profile picture is the YOU the people out there on social media are seeing. If you're laughing on your profile picture, anyone that sees your account or chatting with you might think at that

particular moment you're laughing because that's the image you're showing them of yourself. If your face is frowning on your profile picture, then anyone that sees your profile picture might also think your frowning at that particular time.

How you appear on your profile picture is how people will perceive in their hearts that you in real life anytime they come in contact with your account. That is why you must be careful before choosing your profile pictures.

If you want to use a particular picture as your profile picture, first ask yourself, *is this suitable to be used on a billboard that's talking about me?*

I want to believe you understand that question? A billboard is public and everyone sees it. So first ask yourself if the picture you're about to upload can be used on a billboard that's talking about you. If your answer is yes, then go ahead. If your answer is no, then don't use it.

Let your profile picture be decent.

Don't use pictures that are not decent. The president of your country uses a good picture on his profile. Same with every member of his cabinet. The CEOs of multinational firms use good pictures of themselves on social media. Same with every leader in any organization. The minister of health in your country uses a good and decent picture on his social media, the same with other professionals in your country. I know you want to be greater than them, so appear descent on your profile picture.

Don't use any other thing on your profile picture, make sure is your picture that's there. The picture should look nice. Let it be taken with a good camera, on a good background, and let it show your face clearly.

3. Write a Responsible Bio:
On every social media account, there's always a place provided for you to describe yourself in a few words. This is the section called **Bio**.

The bio is another part of your social media account that talks about you. I've seen a lot of teenagers who write irresponsible bio with emojis that signify wrong things. This is not proper.

Your bio should talk about you, your interest, and maybe your aspirations.

Don't try to copy the bio of someone else who is not going to the same place as you. Be unique in your bio. Let it tell who you are properly.

Examples:
As a teenager, these are some examples of how your Bio should look:

- "A Smart 17-year-old girl with interest in Nature. Aspiring to be a Medical doctor with a great love for Biology"
-
- "16, Interested in Fashion and a Great Lover of Music. Willing to learn from experts"
-
- "18 Years Old With Great passion to serve

humanity as a Lawyer. Very good in literature and government. Always willing to share my thoughts with friends.

●
● An intelligent teenager with an exceptional mindset. Aspiring to be an Economist. I love discussing Economics.

These are examples. You can model any of them and make them suitable for your kind of personality. My interest is to make sure you appear responsible in case a well-meaning personality comes across your profile, he can feel free to connect with you and have a meaningful discussion.

4. Type In Correct English:

I've mentioned this on the previous chapter. I still want to bring it up here again due to its level of importance. Being on social media doesn't mean you should type or chat with incorrect English spellings or grammar. Don't abbreviate. Don't write "k" instead of "Okay", GM instead of "Good Morning", I know there are many others. Don't do such. Type with correct English.

5. Don't Create Multiple Social Media Accounts:

It's an act of irresponsibility to have multiple personal social media accounts on one platform. Have just ONE.

On Facebook, for instance, have just one Facebook account. The purpose is so if anyone hears about you and wants to connects with you, it will be easier for the person to locate you.

If you have many accounts with your name and your picture on them, it makes you look irresponsible because a 21st-century teenager should not be multiple on a social media account.

Most times when I see people create multiple accounts, they tell me they either lost the password of the other one or it was hacked.

Now see, if you lose your password, it's an act of irresponsibility because it shows you can't keep records of yourself properly or you don't even have a retentive memory.

If your account was hacked, that means you're careless. It means you're not careful with your personal property. You didn't pay good attention to secure it. Hence, is either you're not careful of the devices you do log in or you're not careful of what you use as your password.

Let me give you some suggestions here. To make your password strong and *hack-proof* you need to make it very strong. Mix it with capital letters and special characters. For instance, I once managed an account for a church and this is how I coined the password; **"Jesusislord4u@Me."** *Notice the upper case letters.* The full-stop is part of the password. I don't think there's any demon that can crack this. So think in this direction and coin your password.

Don't use your name, your nickname, your date of birth, your father's name, your phone number, or that of any of your relations. Just use **something crazy** as a password and you're secured. If for any reason you use your social media on a friend's device, be careful not to save your password on their browsers and once you're done, make sure you log out.

I believe that helps you.

CONCLUSION
How you appear on social media is how you will be approached. Appear responsibly if you want to be approached responsibly.

NUMBER SIX

10 SOCIAL MEDIA ETHICS YOU MUST KNOW AS A TEENAGER

I will like to share with you some social media ethics you're supposed to know and live by as a teenager.

These ethics will help you with the way you package your lifestyle and relationships with people on social media.

Just like in real life, online ethics are meant to build a very good relationship with people and at the same time, present you as a responsible person. Below are some of the social media ethics:

1. Don't Argue on Social Media
I've seen a lot of people argue on social media. I call them social media debaters. Once a discussion or an idea is not in line with their thought, they argue over it. They argue on the comment session, in groups. They are all across every social media platform including online forums. Most times the argument might lead to insults and online brutalization. Kindly avoid the argument.

If you have a position or thought on a particular subject matter, make your contributions with clear words, proven facts, and sources if possible. Once you're done, leave it. Don't argue or insult anyone just because they don't agree with you.

Allow people to express their views as well and don't argue or insult anyone no matter what the person might have said. Don't come on social media to defend your religious beliefs using insults. Arguments and insults will make no positive impact in any discussion. That's why you need to be polite.

You can never influence anyone you've insulted. You can never make anyone your friend if you've insulted them before on a public domain like social media. Please avoid the argument.

2. Be Slow to Accept Friend Request and Quick to UNFRIEND and BLOCK

On Facebook and LinkedIn for instance, you're not meant to be quick in accepting anyone as a friend. If you go through the person's profile and notice you don't know him/her and he doesn't look like someone you will learn anything from, don't accept the person.

In your friend list, if you notice anyone who is not making sense at all, BLOCK the person. Some might be in your DM talking out of point, don't keep such a person, please block him.

If anyone is making comments with no sense, instead of insulting the person, just ignore the person and block him. It's safer for you to have 150 reasonable people on your social media account than to have 10k fools.

Image source: istockphoto.com

3. Don't Make Your Private Life Public

Most teenagers make the mistake of trying to tell the whole world about themselves on social media. Respect your privacy for your safety.

Starting from when you're setting up your social media, don't make some sensitive information about yourself public. By the way, not every part of the social media you're to supply your information. You can leave some data vacant.

Also, don't post everything you're doing on social media. You're traveling tomorrow, it's on your social media including the transport company/route you will be taking.

You're going to see a friend, you update it. Including where your friend's house is and how to get there.

Mummy scolded you, you went immediately and write it on your status. That's very wrong dear.
Don't make your personal life public. Respect yourself, your family, and your relationships, and do well to keep them away from social media.

4. The Internet Never Forgets. Mind What You Post

This statement, "The Internet never forgets" always keeps me humble on social media. Everything you post online today might be used against you tomorrow especially if you're aspiring to be a public figure.

Image source: vectorstock.com

Before you post anything, ask yourself, will I be comfortable seeing this in the future? If any of my grandchildren should see this, will his/her reaction be positive? If your answer is yes, then go ahead. If your answer is No, then don't. It's a function of self-judgment.

I have seen people who became a celebrity and all of a sudden, what they posted on social media about 10 years ago eventually surfaces and people started using it frustrates their personality and their career. In this case, most of them came out to apologize. It's a pity. They never thought before they posted.

You might think many people don't know you now, but that's not likely to be the story tomorrow. You can be a public figure tomorrow or occupy an enviable position in the future and some enemies and oppositions will start looking for ways to tarnish your image. The only place they can go to is your past posts on social media.
Be careful of what you post. The Internet Never Forgets.

5. Be Careful of The Groups, Conversations, and Trends You Join
If you belong to any group on social media and the group is not impacting you positively then leave that group. Always be quick to leave places that are not necessary on social media. Any group that is teaching what is contrary to your moral upbringing, no matter you added or invited you to the group, kindly leave the group.

If you're in any group that is having discussions you can't easily share with your parents, then that place is not for you.

Also, some social media conversations are not necessary. Not every conversation you join. If your integrity will be at stake for being in a conversation, kindly ignore it. You must not comment on every news, every picture, status update, or on a trending topic/hashtag.

There are times you will see some trending topics and you will perceive in your heart to ignore them. Detectives in several countries now use social media to track criminal suspects. They do this by following the trend of such crime on social media and see what people are saying about it. Anyone with a suspicious comment/post becomes a suspect and in most cases, the person might be innocent just that he commented out of anger or hatred, and it ends up getting him/her into trouble. Maybe by the time they discover the person's innocence, he might have spent days or even months in a police cell.

That's why you must be careful. Not every trending societal you will join. Anyone that has to do with crime or unacceptable or controversial behavior, you have to season your words carefully before you drop a comment on it.

If possible, read what others said and keep scrolling.

6. Always Untag Yourself From Irrelevant Posts

You want to maintain your prestige and good personality on the internet. If anyone tags you on any unnecessary post, kindly untag yourself if the platform allows that. Also, set your privacy very well so that people will not be tagging you on their posts without your approval.

Most people are fond of tagging other people unnecessarily even when the post has nothing to do with the other person. If you're such a person stop it. If you see yourself tagged on such a post then untag yourself. If you notice anyone always tagging you on his/her post and you don't really know the person very well, wisdom demands you warn the person to stop that. The reason is this, if anyone keeps tagging you frequently, it will be assumed that you're very close to the person. So if this is not the case, then ask the person to stop that.

7. Don't Stalk Anyone With False Messages

There are people whose job is to create false messages and spread them to their contacts. The worst of it is they instruct you to send it to 20 people. Not only that. Some will claim is a prayer and that if you don't send it to others, something bad thing will happen to you. If you notice such from a friend, kindly warn the person not to stalk you with such again.

Also, on no account should you do the same to others. Don't spread such an embarrassing broadcast if you want to be seen as responsible.

No one has ever been blessed by spreading a message on social media. If you see messages with such false promises, warn the person that sends it not to do so again and make sure you don't do it to others.

8. Never Disclose Your Personal Issues To a Stranger You Met on Social Media

Meeting different people via social media does not mean you should be completely open to all of them. You're not meant to disclose your personal goals, wins, and challenges to someone you just met on social media.

Most people pretend to be good on social media but in their hearts, their intentions are very bad. Some will come as helpers, as advisers, or as mentors, while in their hearts they're after something.

Whether you're a boy or a girl, don't fall prey to any of these predators. If you notice a particular stranger is trying to get too intimate with you, it's time to either ignore him/her or block him. Don't make yourself cheap to any stranger.

People that have value to add to others don't chase after other people on social media. Men of value are always busy with themselves. So if anyone is so much after you for reasons either you or he can't explain, then ignore them for a while.
Be careful of social media hunters. They're everywhere.

9. Don't post to please or hurt anyone

I have addressed this earlier and I feel I should address it here again. Your social media post should not be intended to please or mock anyone.

Be yourself and post who you really are. That's why your utmost desire now should be to develop and be yourself.

Image source: vectorstock.com

10. Follow only relevant people
I have also said this earlier. If the people you're seeing their updates on your timeline are not adding values to you, then it is time to either unfollow them, unfriend them or block them. The choice is yours. Like Les Brown will always say:

FINALLY!!!

SEE YOU AT THE TOP

One of the greatest minds that has ever lived on earth is the man called Albert Einstein. He made a statement that is always my motivation whenever I'm developing myself on something. He said: *"Try not to become a man of success. Rather become a man of value."*

This is why my concern each time I'm with a teenager like you is always to educate the person on how to add value to himself.

Value is what makes you successful. It is the value that makes a celebrity. Value makes you rich.

That is the essence of this book. My purpose for you is to add value to yourself. There are a lot of distractions today and one of them is social media. If you're not disciplined in the use of social media you might end up spending your time without having anything to show for it.

For each time you spend on social media you make someone richer. It could be the owner of the platform or your network providers. If you spend time on social media learning and building yourself, then you're not losing anything. Remember I said earlier, time wasted can never be regained.

INDEX

Number One
[a] Proverbs 4:23
[b] 1Corithians 15:33
[c] Philippians 4:8

Number Two
[a] 21 Irrefutable Laws of Leadership by John C.
Maxwell
[b] Proverbs 22:29
[c] 2Timothy 2:15

Number Three
[a] Proverbs 23:7

Number Four
[a] 1Corinthians 10:23
[b] Proverbs 29:18
[c] 1Corinthians 10:23

Number Five
Proverbs 4:7

ABOUT THE AUTHOR

Chukwuma Gordian is a Nigerian-born entrepreneur, sales and marketing expert, speaker, and corporate trainer. He is the founder of Chux Global Resources, a Nigerian-based organization that specializes in the importation and distribution of beauty products and smart security gadgets.

His greatest passion is to see people grow, discover their hidden potentials, and make enviable exploits. He is a lover of teenagers.

If you will like to connect with him, you can do so using any of the followings channels:

Website: chumagordian.com

Facebook, Instagram, Twitter and Tiktok:
@chumagordian

LinkedIn and YouTube:
Chukwuma Gordian

Email:
hello@chumagordian.com

Printed in Great Britain
by Amazon

44218684R00059